W9-CCN-377

Little Apple

A Book of Thanks

Brigitte Weninger

Anne Möller

No part of this publication may be reproduced in whole or in part, or stored
in a retrieval system, or transmitted in any form or by any means, electronic,
mechanical, photocopying, recording, or otherwise, without written permission of
the publisher. For information regarding permission, write to North-South Books,
Inc., 1123 Broadway, Suite 800, New York, NY 10010.

ISBN 0-439-32550-1

Copyright © 2001 by Michael Neugebauer Verlag, an imprint of Nord-Sud Verlag
AG, Gossau Zürich, Switzerland. First published in Switzerland under the title
Danke, kleiner Apfel! English translation copyright © 2001 by North-South Books,
Inc. All rights reserved. Published by Scholastic Inc., 555 Broadway, New York,
NY 10012, by arrangement North-South Books, Inc. SCHOLASTIC and associated
logos are trademarks and/or registered trademarks of Scholastic Inc.

12 11 10 9 8 7 6 5 4 3 2 1   1 2 3 4 5 6/0

Printed in the U.S.A.   09

First Scholastic printing, September 2001

Little Apple

A Book of Thanks

SCHOLASTIC INC.
New York Toronto London Auckland Sydney
Mexico City New Delhi Hong Kong Buenos Aires

Look at this little apple.
It is so round and smooth and pretty.

Some apples are red, others yellow or green —and some are all three!

Apples are sweet, juicy, and very good for you.
Even the birds know that!

If you cut open an apple,
you will discover a secret:
There's a little star
hidden inside!

In this little star are the brown apple pips.

If you plant one of the little pips in damp earth, it wakes up. It swells and bulges, then takes root and a shoot grows out of it.

In a few years the little shoot becomes
a beautiful apple tree.

In spring the tree is covered with
delicate pinkish-white apple blossoms.
Many bees come to sip the blossoms' nectar.
As they do, they carry pollen from
blossom to blossom.

In summer the blossoms turn into young fruit.
Every day they grow a little bigger and rounder.

Rich earth and warm rain help them to grow,
and the warm sun makes them sweet and juicy.
By autumn they are delicious ripe apples.

The farmer picks them from the tree.

And then I have an apple to eat.
I hope that other children have healthy
fruit to eat, too.
I am so thankful for this little apple.